Unsent, but not Unspoken

TIGRESS

Copyright © 2025 by Tigress

All rights reserved.

No part of this publication may be reproduced, stored in a retrieval system, or transmitted in any form or by any means—electronic, mechanical, photocopying, recording, or otherwise—without prior written permission from the publisher, except in brief quotations used for reviews or scholarly works.

This journal is an original creative work. Any references to individuals, events, or places are used illustratively. Any resemblance to actual persons, living or deceased, is purely coincidental.

Published by **Tigress Sounds & Publishing Inc.**

New York, USA

First Edition: 2025

For more information about our books, visit: www.TigressPublishing.com

Cover Design by Tigress

Printed in the United States of America

Unsent, But Not Unspoken

Written by Tigress

Illustrated by Tigress

A NOTE TO THE READER

Not all letters need a mailbox.
This journal is a space for the words you were never able to speak-because it wasn't safe, or you weren't ready, or there was simply no one to hear them.
Here, you write without filters. Without fear. Without needing a reply.
Because sometimes, healing begins not with what is sent, but with what is finally said.
Let your voice take up space. It always deserved to.

LETTERS TO THE ONE WHO HURT ME

A letter I never sent because I was scared

Date:

Write what fear once held back. Say what you couldn't then, now.

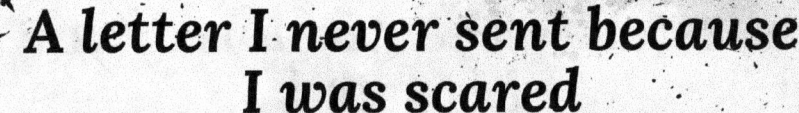

A letter to the version of you I trusted

Date:

Speak to the part of them you once believed in. What do you need to say to that memory?

A letter I wanted to send, but didn't

Date:

This is the message that stayed stuck inside. Let it breathe now.

A letter that starts with "How dare you..."

Date:

Begin with the boldness you once buried. This is your space to be unfiltered.

A letter that ends with "But I forgive myself"

Date:

Release what you carried. Let the weight go where it belongs—off of you.

LETTERS TO THE ONE I LOST

A letter to the person I never got to say goodbye to

Write the goodbye you never got to give. Let this be the closure that never came.

Date:

A letter to someone who left without explanation

Date:

What do you say when silence was all they left behind? Say it here.

A letter to the ghost that still walks through my mind

Date:

Speak to the memory that lingers. It's time to name what still haunts you.

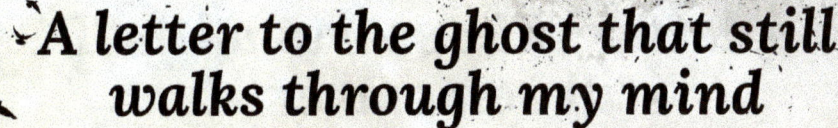

A letter that starts with "I still remember..."

Date:

Let memory take the lead. Begin with what never left your heart.

A letter to the silence that came after you

Date:

There's pain in what wasn't said. Write to the void that followed them.

LETTERS TO THE ONE I USED TO BE

A letter to the me who stayed too long

Write to the version of you who didn't yet know how to walk away. Let her feel seen.

Date:

A letter to the me who never spoke up

Date:

Speak for the silenced version of you. Give her the words she once held back.

A letter to the inner child who waited for love

Date:

Talk to the little one who longed to be chosen. Remind her she is enough.

A letter that starts with "You didn't deserve that..."

Begin with what was unfair. Let this be a letter of truth and tenderness.

Date:

A letter to the me who finally walked away

Date: _____

Celebrate her. Thank her. She saved you.

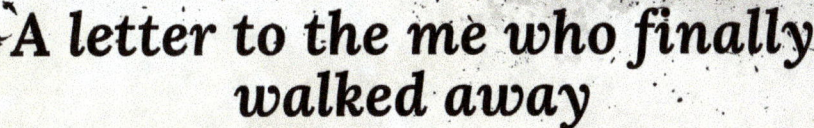

_____
_____
_____
_____
_____
_____
_____
_____
_____
_____
_____
_____
_____
_____
_____
_____
_____
_____
_____
_____
_____
_____
_____
_____

LETTERS TO WHAT WAS NEVER SAID

A letter to the apology I'll never hear

Date: _____

Write the words they never gave you. You don't need them to move forward.

_____
_____
_____
_____
_____
_____
_____
_____
_____
_____
_____
_____
_____
_____
_____
_____
_____
_____
_____
_____
_____
_____
_____
_____
_____

A letter to the love I couldn't name

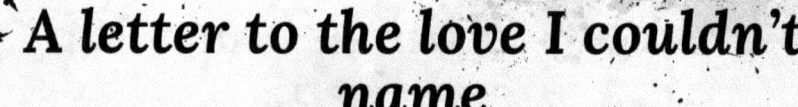

Speak to the feelings you couldn't explain, but still felt deeply.

Date:
_____

A letter to the truth I hid

Date:

Name the secret. Let it be known on your terms.

A letter to the pain I carried in silence

Date:

Give voice to the ache you endured alone. Let this be your release.

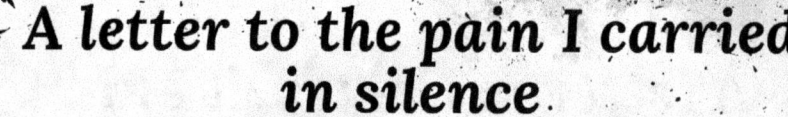

A letter that ends with "Now I'm free"

Date:

Close this one with liberation. You don't need permission to let go.

LETTERS THAT SET ME FREE

A letter to the anger I buried

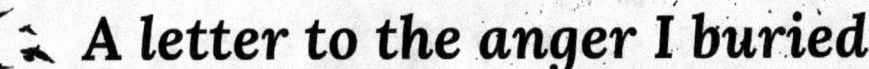

Date:

What fury did you swallow? Dig it up and write it down. You're allowed to feel it.

A letter to my own strength

Date:

Write to the part of you that got back up, even when no one saw it.

A letter to the part of me that survived

Date:

Speak to the one who endured. Remind her she made it.

A letter that begins with "I release..."

Date:

Let go. Of what you carried. Of what you were never meant to hold.

A final letter — to anyone, for anything

Date:

This one is yours, entirely. To whomever. For whatever. Because your words matter.

AFFIRMATIONS

- I do not need permission to heal.
- My truth is valid, even if no one ever reads it
- I am not broken. I am becoming.

TEAR & BURN RELEASE RITUAL

- This page is not meant to last.
- Use it to write the final word of grief, of
- anger, of hope, of goodbye.
- Then tear it out. Burn it (safely). Bury it. Rip it into pieces.
- Let this be the end of what no longer belongs to you.

CERTIFICATE OF COURAGE

Awarded to: _____

Date: _____

- For giving your truth a voice.
- For writing what silence never could.
- For putting emotion to paper, and pain into purpose.
- You chose expression over erasure.
- You didn't need a reply—only the courage to begin.

Prepared by: Tigress

CLOSING MESSAGE

You wrote what you were never allowed to say.
You put into words what once sat like a stone
in your chest.

They may never know But now you do..
You weren't voiceless. Just waiting for the page.

And now, it's here.
You are free.

SOME LETTERS ARE NEVER SENT.
BUT THE WORDS STILL CARRY WEIGHT.

THIS JOURNAL IS YOUR QUIET CONFESSIONAL—
A PLACE TO SAY WHAT YOU NEVER COULD,
TO POUR TRUTH INTO INK,
AND GIVE VOICE TO THE SILENCE YOU'VE CARRIED.

LET IT BE WRITTEN, EVEN IF NEVER DELIVERED.

www.ingramcontent.com/pod-product-compliance
Lightning Source LLC
Chambersburg PA
CBHW050518100526
44581CB00001B/21